Delicious lunches

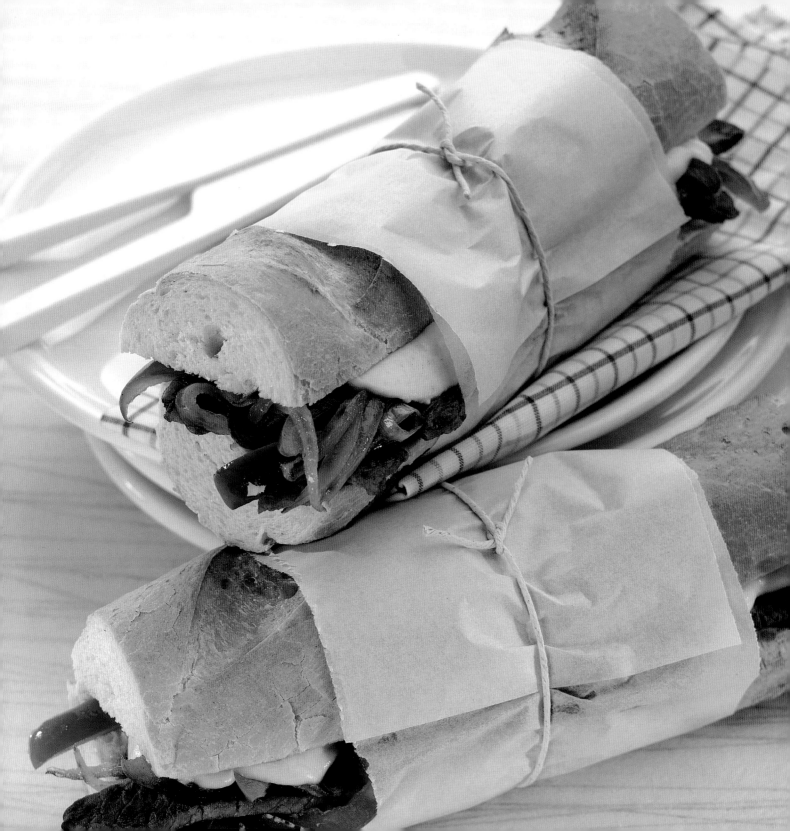

Delicious
lunches

Love Food ™ is an imprint of Parragon Books Ltd

Parragon
Queen Street House
4 Queen Street
Bath BA1 1HE, UK

Cover and internal design by Mark Cavanagh
Introduction by Bridget Jones
Photography by Don Last
Home Economist Christine Last

ISBN 978-1-4054-9270-6
Printed in China

Notes for the reader
• This book uses imperial, metric and US cup measurements. Follow the same units of measurements throughout; do not mix imperial and metric.
• All spoon measurements are level: teaspoons are assumed to be 5 ml, and tablespoons are assumed to be 15 ml.
• Unless otherwise stated, milk is assumed to be low fat and eggs are medium. The times given are an approximate guide only.
• Some recipes contain nuts. If you are allergic to nuts you should avoid using them and any products containing nuts. Recipes using raw or very lightly cooked eggs should be avoided by infants, the elderly, pregnant women, convalescents, and anyone suffering from illness.

Contents

Lunches

There are those who "lunch" and for whom midday dining is a status symbol in terms of where, rather than what. For most, lunch means everything from potato chips to business meetings, hot dogs to food fiesta. Snacking or celebrating, lunch is about making the most of an array of eating. Don't miss out—enjoy!

Snack attack

Hunger pangs: no plans, no time, and no lunch allowance? It's too easy to grab a commercial snack-pack and fall into the lousy lunch routine. Take a fresh look at lunch box options for all the family, whatever they may be doing at work, school, after the game, or together for an outing.

• Leafy salads stay fresh when the dressing is packed separately.

• Pasta, potatoes, beans, and pulses make good prepare-ahead lunches.

• Crunchy nuts and seeds go well with couscous or rice bases, as well as most other salads.

• Shredded roots and shoots travel well—carrots, celery root, or beet, and bean sprouts.

Sandwich world

Sandwiches can be brilliant every day. Keep fillings light, such as canned tuna fish, lean roast beef, wafer-thin cooked ham, smoked chicken or turkey, finely shredded cheese, vegetable-based fillings. Delicate open sandwiches with stylish toppings are smart for leisurely lunches.

• Bagels, French, wraps, pumpernickel, rye, whole wheat or mixed grain—use all breads, not the same each day. Slice them thickly to satisfy appetites with carbohydrate rather than too much fat.

• Cut the fat for everyday eating. Butter isn't always essential and thick-spread mayo should be a rare

treat. Try brushing olive, walnut or pistachio oil lightly over thick breads; use low fat soft cheese to spread; spread full-flavored pesto finely; or use peanut (or other nut) butter thinly.

• Major on finely cut vegetables—bell peppers, zucchini, cabbage, tomatoes, cucumber, fennel, celery, or carrot.

Just a light bite?

When supper is going to be special, satisfy midday hunger pangs with a combination of light foods (salad, fruit, a dip, and crudités) and a nutritious drink. In winter, light broths and smooth soups are a good choice. Homemade, they can be reheated rapidly in the microwave. Carry them in a vacuum flask for a warming lunch away from home.

Lunchtime celebrations

Lunch is the perfect time to bring friends and family together for a relaxed celebration that can be smart and slightly formal or simply fun.

• Allow gathering time for everyone to arrive and relax. Provide nibbles merely to whet the appetite. Don't expect guests to leave promptly: plan to round off over several pots of coffee or refreshing afternoon tea.

• Sit-down lunches are unrushed. Linger over and between courses. Plan a menu that will not spoil—include cook-aheads and desserts that go from chiller to table.

• Get everyone involved for informal fun: try self-service from kitchen countertops, cook together, Swiss fondue, or barbecue.

• Pre-lunch alcohol can be potent, so offer soft drinks and fruit cups. Keep wines light. Have plenty of water. Cater for children and drivers.

• For larger gatherings, try to invite people who know each other or in groups. Lone children soon get bored and it's a good idea to arrange entertainment to keep the youngsters occupied, allowing parents to relax.

1

Lunch Box

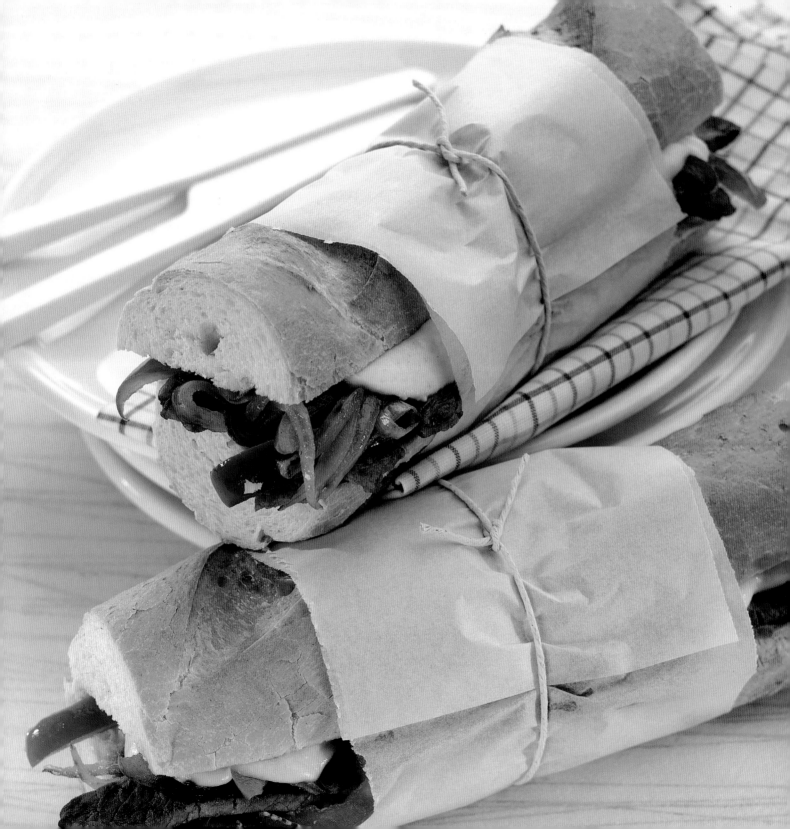

serves 4

1 baguette

12 oz/350 g boneless rib-eye
steak, partially frozen

3 tbsp olive oil

1 onion, thinly sliced

1 green bell pepper,
thinly sliced

salt and pepper

$2^3/4$ oz/75 g provolone or
mozzarella cheese,
thinly sliced

cheese steak baguette

Cut the bread into 4 equal lengths, then cut each piece
horizontally in half. Thinly slice the partially frozen steak
across the grain.

Heat 2 tablespoons of the oil in a large skillet over medium
heat, add the onion and green bell pepper, and cook, stirring
occasionally, for 10–15 minutes until softened and golden
brown. Push the mixture to one side of the skillet.

Heat the remaining oil in the skillet over medium heat. When
hot, add the steak, and stir-fry for 4–5 minutes until tender. Stir
the onion mixture and steak together and season to taste with
salt and pepper.

Preheat the broiler to medium. Divide the steak mixture among
the 4 bottom halves of bread and top with the cheese. Broil for
1–2 minutes until the cheese has melted, then cover with the top
halves of bread and press down gently. Serve at once, or wrap in
wax paper or foil for a lunch box.

serves 4

1 baguette

butter, for spreading

mixed salad greens

3 tbsp olive oil

2 onions, thinly sliced

1 lb 8 oz/675 g rump or
sirloin steak, about 1 inch/
2.5 cm thick

salt and pepper

1 tbsp Worcestershire sauce

2 tbsp wholegrain mustard

2 tbsp water

mustard steak baguette

Cut the bread into 4 equal lengths, then cut each piece horizontally in half. Spread each half with some butter and add a few salad greens to the bottom halves.

Heat 2 tablespoons of the oil in a large, heavy-bottom skillet over medium heat. Add the onions and cook, stirring occasionally, for 10–15 minutes until softened and golden brown. Using a slotted spoon, transfer to a plate and set aside.

Increase the heat to high and add the remaining oil to the skillet. When hot, add the steak, season to taste with pepper, and cook quickly on both sides to seal. Reduce the heat to medium and cook, turning once, for 2½–3 minutes each side for rare or 3½–5 minutes each side for medium. Transfer the steak to the plate with the onions.

Add the Worcestershire sauce, mustard, and water to the skillet and stir to deglaze by scraping any sediment from the bottom of the skillet. Return the onions to the skillet, season to taste with salt and pepper, and mix well.

Thinly slice the steak across the grain, divide it among the 4 bottom halves of bread, and cover with the onion mixture. Cover with the top halves of bread and press down gently. Serve at once, or wrap in wax paper or foil for a lunch box.

serves 4

4 oz/115 g mozzarella cheese, grated

4 oz/115 g Cheddar cheese, grated

8 oz/225 g cooked chorizo sausage (outer casing removed) or ham, diced

4 scallions, finely chopped

2 fresh green chiles, such as poblano, seeded and finely chopped

salt and pepper

8 flour tortillas

vegetable oil, for brushing

lime wedges, to garnish

guacamole and salsa, to serve

chorizo & cheese quesadillas

Place the cheeses, chorizo, scallions, chiles, and salt and pepper to taste in a bowl and mix together.

Divide the mixture among 4 of the flour tortillas, then top with the remaining tortillas.

Brush a large, nonstick or heavy-bottom skillet with oil and heat over medium heat. Add 1 quesadilla and cook, pressing it down with a spatula, for 4–5 minutes until the underside is crisp and lightly browned. Turn over and cook the other side until the cheese is melting. Remove from the skillet and keep warm. Cook the remaining quesadilla.

Cut each quesadilla into quarters, arrange on a warmed serving plate and serve accompanied by some guacamole and salsa. If eating away from the home, wrap the quesadillas in wax paper or foil, and transport the guacamole and salsa in airtight containers.

serves 2

1 large egg, hard-cooked and cooled

7 oz/200 g canned tuna in spring water, drained

7 oz/200 g canned no-added-sugar corn kernels, drained

2 wholewheat flour tortillas

1 carton of mustard cress

for the dressing

1 tbsp plain yogurt

1 tsp olive oil

1/2 tsp white wine vinegar

1/2 tsp Dijon mustard

pepper

tortillas with tuna, egg & corn

To make the dressing, whisk the yogurt, oil, vinegar, and mustard, and pepper to taste, in a pitcher until emulsified and smooth.

Shell the egg, separate the yolk and the white, then mash the yolk and mince the white. Mash the tuna with the egg and dressing, then mix in the corn.

Spread the filling equally over the 2 tortillas and sprinkle over the mustard cress. Fold in one end and roll up. Wrap in wax paper for a lunch box.

serves 4

scant ¹/2 cup grated carrot

2 oz/55 g white cabbage,
thinly sliced

¹/3 cup plain yogurt

1 tsp cider vinegar

¹/8 cup raisins

7 oz/200 g canned tuna steak
in water, drained

2 tbsp pumpkin seeds

freshly ground black pepper

4 wholewheat or white
pita breads

4 eating apples, to serve

raisin coleslaw & tuna-filled pita breads

Mix the carrot, cabbage, yogurt, vinegar, and raisins together in a bowl. Lightly stir in the tuna and half the pumpkin seeds and season to taste with pepper.

Lightly toast the pita breads under a preheated hot broiler or in a toaster, then let cool slightly. Using a sharp knife, cut each pita bread in half to make pockets. Divide the filling evenly among the pita breads. Core the apples and cut into wedges, then serve at once with the filled pita breads.

If you are planning on eating this away from the home, prepare the filled pita breads as described above and wrap well in wax paper. The apple should be kept whole and cut into wedges just before you plan to eat.

serves 2

2–4 pita breads

1 tbsp olive oil

1 tsp vinegar

1/2 tsp Dijon mustard

pepper

1/4 iceberg lettuce, finely shredded

1 scallion, chopped

1/2 yellow bell pepper, seeded and chopped

1 large tomato, seeded and chopped

2-inch/5-cm piece cucumber, chopped

1 carrot, peeled and grated

for the hummus

14 oz/400 g canned chickpeas, drained and liquid set aside

1 garlic clove, chopped

2 tbsp olive oil

2 tbsp sesame seed paste

juice of 1/2 lemon

pepper

pinch of paprika

pita pockets with hummus & salad

To make the hummus, put the chickpeas, garlic, oil, sesame seed paste, lemon juice, and a little of the chickpea liquid in a blender or food processor and blend until smooth and creamy. Season to taste with pepper and the paprika.

If serving at home, heat the pita breads according to the package directions and cut them in half to create pockets.

To make the dressing, whisk the remaining oil with the vinegar and mustard, and pepper to taste, in a pitcher.

Mix all the salad ingredients together in a bowl, add the dressing, and toss well to coat. Spread the inside of the pita pockets with the hummus, fill with the salad, and serve. For a lunch box, spread the inside of the unheated pita pockets with hummus, fill with the undressed salad, and wrap well in wax paper.

serves 4

4 large baking potatoes

9 oz/250 g cooked skinless, boneless chicken breasts, cubed

4 scallions, sliced thickly

1 cup soft cheese

pepper

mixed salad, to serve

baked potatoes with chicken

Scrub the potatoes and prick them all over with a fork. Bake in a preheated oven, 400°F/200°C, for about 60 minutes, until tender, or cook in a microwave on high power for 12–15 minutes.

Mix the chicken and scallions with the soft cheese.

Cut a cross into the top of each potato and squeeze slightly apart. Spoon the chicken filling into the potatoes and season with black pepper to taste. Serve immediately with a mixed salad.

If you plan to eat this away from home, bake the potato as described above and leave to cool before wrapping in foil. The filling can also be prepared at home and transported in an airtight container.

serves 2

4 slices walnut bread or pain Poilâne, about 1/2 inch/ 1 cm thick

4 thin slices cured ham, such as Bayonne or prosciutto

2 ripe dessert pears, such as Conference, peeled, halved, cored, and thinly sliced lengthways

3 1/2 oz/100 g Roquefort cheese, very thinly sliced

mixed salad greens

walnut vinaigrette

pear & roquefort open sandwiches

Preheat the broiler to high. Put the bread slices under the broiler and toast until crisp, but not brown, on both sides. Do not turn off the broiler.

Fold or cut the ham slices to cover each slice of bread, then divide the pear slices equally among them. Lay the cheese slices on top.

Return the open sandwiches to the grill until the cheese melts and bubbles. Mix the salad greens with the walnut vinaigrette and serve 1 or 2 open sandwiches each with the salad on the side.

If you want to eat this away from the home, perhaps at work, you can prepare this in the same way providing you have access to a toaster. It's not essential that the cheese is melted, so the separate ingredients can be transported in individual airtight containers.

serves 2

2 leeks

2 tbsp butter

1 cup grated Gruyère cheese

2 scallions, finely chopped

1 tbsp chopped fresh parsley

salt and pepper

2 fresh bagels

bagels with leeks & cheese

Trim the leeks, discarding the green ends, and split down the center, leaving the root intact. Wash well to remove any grit and slice finely, discarding the root.

Melt the butter over low heat in a large sauté pan and add the leeks. Cook, stirring constantly, for 5 minutes, or until the leeks are soft and slightly browned. Let cool.

Preheat the broiler. Mix the cooled leeks, grated cheese, scallions, parsley, and salt and pepper to taste together. Split the bagels and toast lightly on the bottom. Spread the cheese mixture over the top of each bagel and place under the preheated broiler until bubbling and golden brown.

You can eat this away from the home, perhaps at work, if you have access to a toaster. The topping can be prepared at home and transported in an airtight container. The toasted bagels can be eaten with the topping served at room temperature.

serves 2

3 wholewheat bread English muffins, halved

2 tbsp tomato paste

2 tbsp pesto

1 tbsp olive oil

1/2 red onion, thinly sliced

3 mushrooms, sliced

1/2 zucchini, thinly sliced

2–3 slices ham or 6 slices salami

scant 1 cup grated Cheddar cheese or 6 slices mozzarella cheese

cherry tomatoes, to serve (optional)

mini muffin pizzas

Toast the muffins until golden, then let cool.

Mix the tomato paste and pesto together in a small bowl and spread equally over the muffin halves.

Heat the oil in a nonstick skillet and then cook the onion, mushrooms, and zucchini until soft and beginning to brown.

Preheat the broiler to high. Divide the vegetables between the muffins, top with the ham, then the cheese.

Cook under the broiler for 3–4 minutes until the cheese is melted and browned. Serve hot or cold with cherry tomatoes if desired. Wrap in wax paper for a lunch box.

2

Lunchtime Specials

serves 4

12 slices French bread or rustic bread

4 tbsp olive oil

2 garlic cloves, chopped

2 tbsp finely chopped fresh oregano

salt and pepper

3½ oz/100 g cold roast chicken, cut into small, thin slices

4 tomatoes, sliced

12 thin slices of goat cheese

12 black olives, pitted and chopped

fresh green salad leaves, to serve

chicken crostini

Preheat the oven to 350°F/180°C and the broiler to medium. Put the bread under the preheated broiler and lightly toast on both sides. Meanwhile, pour the olive oil into a bowl and add the garlic and oregano. Season with salt and pepper and mix well. Remove the toasted bread slices from the broiler and brush them on one side only with the oil mixture.

Place the bread slices, oiled sides up, on a cookie sheet. Put some sliced chicken on top of each one, followed by a slice of tomato. Divide the slices of goat cheese between them, then top with the chopped olives. Drizzle over the remaining oil mixture and transfer to the preheated oven. Bake for about 5 minutes, or until the cheese is golden and starting to melt. Remove from the oven and serve with fresh green salad leaves.

serves 4

1 small oval-shaped loaf of
white bread (ciabatta
or bloomer)

125 ml/4 fl oz extra-virgin
olive oil

4 tomatoes

6 leaves fresh basil

salt and pepper

8 black olives, stoned and
chopped (optional)

1 large garlic clove

tomato & basil bruschetta

Cut the bread into ½-inch/1-cm slices. Pour half of the oil into
a shallow dish and place the bread in it. Leave for 2–3 minutes,
turn and leave for 2 more minutes, or until thoroughly saturated
in oil.

Meanwhile, seed and dice the tomatoes and place in a mixing
bowl. Tear the basil leaves and sprinkle over the tomatoes.
Season with salt and pepper. Add the olives, if using. Pour over
the remaining olive oil and leave to marinate.

Preheat the griddle over a medium heat. Cook the bread until
golden and crispy on both sides (about 2 minutes on each side).
Remove the bread from the griddle and arrange on an attractive
serving dish.

Peel the garlic clove and cut in half. Rub the cut edge over the
surface of the bruschetta. Top each slice with a spoonful of
the tomato mixture and serve.

serves 4

1 lb/450 g best ground steak

4 onions

2–4 garlic cloves, crushed

2–3 tsp grated fresh
horseradish or 1–1$^{1}/_{2}$ tbsp
creamed horseradish

pepper

8 lean Canadian bacon slices

2 tbsp corn oil

sesame seeded buns, to serve

green salad leaves, to garnish

the ultimate steak & bacon burger

Place the ground steak in a large bowl. Finely grate 1 of the onions and add to the ground steak in the bowl.

Add the garlic, horseradish, and pepper to the steak mixture in the bowl. Mix together, then shape into 4 equal-size burgers. Wrap each burger in 2 slices of bacon, then cover and let chill for 30 minutes.

Preheat the broiler to medium-high. Slice the remaining onions. Heat the oil in a skillet. Add the onions and cook over medium heat for 8–10 minutes, stirring frequently, until the onions are golden brown. Drain on paper towels and keep warm.

Cook the burgers under the hot broiler for 3–5 minutes on each side or until cooked to personal preference. Serve inside sesame seeded buns with a spoonful of the fried onions and a green salad garnish.

serves 4

2 tbsp sunflower-seed oil, plus extra for oiling

finely grated rind of 1 lime

1 tbsp lime juice

2 garlic cloves, crushed

$1/4$ tsp ground coriander

$1/4$ tsp ground cumin

pinch of sugar

salt and pepper

1 piece rump steak, about 1 lb 8 oz/675 g and $3/4$ inch/ 2 cm thick

4 tortillas

1 avocado

2 tomatoes, thinly sliced

4 tbsp sour cream

4 scallions, thinly sliced

cilantro sprigs and lime wedges, to garnish

grilled steak fajitas

To make the marinade, put the oil, lime rind and juice, garlic, coriander, cumin, sugar, and salt and pepper to taste into a large, shallow, nonmetallic dish large enough to hold the steak and mix together. Add the steak and turn in the marinade to coat it. Cover and let marinate in the refrigerator for 6–8 hours or up to 24 hours, turning occasionally.

When ready to cook, preheat the broiler. Using a slotted spoon, remove the steak from the marinade, put onto an oiled broiler or grill rack, and cook under medium heat for 5 minutes for rare or 8–10 minutes for medium, turning the steak frequently and basting once or twice with any remaining marinade.

Meanwhile, warm the tortillas according to the instructions on the package. Peel, pit, and slice the avocado.

Thinly slice the steak across the grain and arrange an equal quantity of the slices on one side of each tortilla. Add the tomato and avocado slices, top with a spoonful of sour cream, and sprinkle over the scallions. Fold over and serve garnished with cilantro sprigs and lime wedges. Serve at once.

serves 4–8

1 lb 2 oz/500 g large flat mushrooms

2 tbsp oil

1 onion, sliced

1 red bell pepper, seeded and sliced

1 green bell pepper, seeded and sliced

1 garlic clove, crushed

1/4–1/2 tsp cayenne pepper

juice and grated rind of 2 limes

2 tsp sugar

1 tsp dried oregano

salt and pepper

8 flour tortillas

salsa, to serve

mushroom fajitas

Cut the mushrooms into strips. Heat the oil in a large, heavy-bottom skillet. Add the mushrooms, onion, red and green bell pepper, and garlic and stir-fry for 8–10 minutes, until the vegetables are cooked.

Add the cayenne pepper, lime juice and rind, sugar, and oregano. Season to taste with salt and pepper and cook for an additional 2 minutes.

Meanwhile, heat the tortillas according to the package instructions. Divide the mushroom mixture

serves 4–6

1/2 cup bulgur wheat

salt and pepper

10 1/2 oz/300 g canned red kidney beans, drained and rinsed

10 1/2 oz/300 g canned cannellini beans, drained

1–2 fresh red jalapeño chiles, seeded and coarsely chopped

2–3 garlic cloves

6 scallions, coarsely chopped

1 yellow bell pepper, seeded, peeled, and chopped

1 tbsp chopped fresh cilantro

4 oz/115 g mature Cheddar cheese, grated

2 tbsp wholewheat flour

1–2 tbsp corn oil

1 large tomato, sliced

wholewheat buns, to serve

vegetarian chile burgers

Cook the bulgur wheat in a pan of lightly salted water for 12 minutes, or until cooked. Drain and set aside.

Place the beans in a food processor with the chiles, garlic, scallions, pepper, cilantro, and half the cheese. Using the pulse button, chop finely. Add to the cooked bulgur wheat with salt and pepper to taste. Mix well, then shape into 4–6 equal-size burgers. Cover and let chill for 1 hour. Coat the burgers in the flour.

Preheat the broiler to medium. Heat a heavy-bottom skillet and add the oil. When hot, add the burgers and cook over medium heat for 5–6 minutes on each side or until piping hot.

Place 1–2 slices of tomato on top of each burger and sprinkle with the remaining cheese. Cook under the hot broiler for 2–3 minutes, or until the cheese starts to melt. Serve in wholewheat buns.

serves 1

2 large eggs

2 tbsp milk

salt and pepper

3/8 stick butter

1 sprig fresh flat-leaf parsley, stem bruised

leaves from 1 sprig of fresh flat-leaf parsley

1 sprig fresh chervil

2 fresh chives

buttered bread, to serve

mixed herb omelet

Break the eggs into a bowl. Add the milk and salt and pepper to taste, and beat quickly until just blended.

Heat an 8-inch/20-cm omelet pan or skillet over medium-high heat until it is very hot and you can feel the heat rising from the surface. Add 1/4 stick of the butter and rub it over the base and around the sides as it melts.

As soon as the butter stops sizzling, pour in the eggs. Shake the pan forward and backward over the heat and use the fork to stir the eggs around the pan in a circular motion. Do not scrape the bottom of the pan.

As the omelet begins to set, use the fork to push the cooked egg from the edge toward the center, so the remaining uncooked egg comes in contact with the hot base of the pan. Continue doing this for 3 minutes, or until the omelet looks set on the bottom, but is still slightly runny on top.

Place the herbs in the center of the omelet. Tilt the pan away from the handle, so the omelet slides toward the edge of the pan. Use the fork to fold the top half of the omelet over the herbs. Slice the omelet onto a plate, then rub the remaining butter over the top and serve with buttered bread. Omelets are best eaten immediately.

serves 2

for the dough

1 1/2 cups all-purpose flour,
plus extra for dusting

1 tsp salt

1 tsp active dry yeast

1 tbsp olive oil, plus extra
for brushing

6 tbsp lukewarm water

for the topping

6 tomatoes, sliced thinly

6 oz mozzarella cheese,
drained and sliced thinly

salt and pepper

2 tbsp shredded basil, plus
extra to garnish

2 tbsp olive oil

cheese & tomato pizza

To make the pizza dough, sift the flour and salt into a bowl and stir in the yeast. Make a well in the center and pour in the oil and water. Gradually incorporate the dry ingredients into the liquid, using a wooden spoon or floured hands.

Turn out the dough onto a lightly floured counter and knead well for 5 minutes, until smooth and elastic. Return to the clean bowl, covered with lightly oiled plastic wrap, and set aside to rise in a warm place for about 1 hour, or until doubled in size.

Turn out the dough onto a lightly floured counter and knock back. Knead briefly, then cut it in half and roll out each piece into a circle about 1/4 inch thick. Transfer to a lightly oiled baking sheet and push up the edges with your fingers to form a small rim.

For the topping, arrange the tomato and mozzarella slices alternately over the pizza base. Season to taste with salt and pepper, sprinkle with the basil, and drizzle with the olive oil.

Bake in a preheated oven, 450°F/230°C, for 15–20 minutes, until the crust is crisp and the cheese has melted. Serve at once, garnished with shredded basil.

serves 2

4 slices ciabatta bread,
lightly toasted

7 oz/200 g feta cheese

2 tbsp olive oil, plus extra
for drizzling

1 tsp dried red chile flakes

1 tsp dried oregano

scant 2 cups arugula leaves,
to serve

broiled feta cheese with chile on ciabatta toast

Preheat the broiler to hot. Place the toasted ciabatta slices on a baking sheet and cover each with a generous slice of feta cheese. Mix the oil, red chile flakes, and oregano together and drizzle evenly over the cheese.

Cook under the preheated broiler for 2–3 minutes, or until the cheese starts to melt, and place on serving plates. Drizzle over a little extra oil and serve with arugula leaves.

serves 4

1 lb 8 oz/675 g large potatoes

sunflower-seed, corn, or peanut oil, for deep-frying

salt and pepper

french fries

Peel the potatoes and cut into ⅜-inch/8-mm even-size fingers. As soon as they are prepared, put them into a large bowl of cold water to prevent discoloration, then let them soak for 30 minutes to remove the excess starch.

Drain the potatoes and dry well on a clean dish towel. Heat the oil in a deep-fryer or large, heavy-bottom pan to 375°F/190°C. If you do not have a thermometer, test the temperature by dropping a potato finger into the oil. If it sinks, the oil isn't hot enough; if it floats and the oil bubbles around it, it is ready. Carefully add a small batch of potatoes to the oil (this is to ensure even cooking and to avoid reducing the temperature of the oil) and deep-fry for 5–6 minutes until soft but not browned. Remove from the oil and drain well on paper towels. Let cool for at least 5 minutes. Continue to deep-fry the remaining potatoes in the same way, allowing the oil to return to the correct temperature each time.

When ready to serve, reheat the oil to 400°F/200°C. Add the potatoes, in small batches, and deep-fry for 2–3 minutes until golden brown. Remove from the oil and drain on paper towels. Serve at once, seasoned to taste with salt and pepper.

Light Lunch

serves 4

3 celery stalks, sliced thinly

1/2 cucumber, sliced thinly

2 scallions, sliced thinly

9 oz/250 g young
spinach leaves

3 tbsp chopped fresh parsley

12 oz/350 g boneless roast
chicken, sliced thinly

for the dressing

1-inch/2.5-cm piece of fresh
gingerroot, grated finely

3 tbsp olive oil

1 tbsp white wine vinegar

1 tbsp honey

1/2 tsp ground cinnamon

salt and pepper

smoked almonds, to garnish
(optional)

chicken & spinach salad

Toss the celery, cucumber, and scallions in a large bowl with the spinach leaves and parsley.

Transfer to serving plates and arrange the chicken on top of the salad.

In a screw-topped jar, combine all the dressing ingredients, including salt and pepper to taste, shake well to mix, and pour it over the salad. Sprinkle with a few smoked almonds, if using.

serves 4

1 lb 10 oz/750 g beef fillet, trimmed of any visible fat

pepper

2 tsp Worcestershire sauce

3 tbsp olive oil

14 oz/400 g green beans

3½ oz/100 g small pasta, such as orecchiette

2 red onions, finely sliced

1 large head radicchio

¼ cup green olives, pitted

scant ⅓ cup shelled hazelnuts, whole

for the dressing

1 tsp Dijon mustard

2 tbsp white wine vinegar

5 tbsp olive oil

roast beef salad

Preheat the oven to 425°F/220°C. Rub the beef with pepper to taste and Worcestershire sauce. Heat 2 tablespoons of the oil in a small roasting pan over high heat, add the beef, and sear on all sides. Transfer the dish to the preheated oven and roast for 30 minutes. Remove and let cool.

Bring a large pan of water to a boil, add the beans, and cook for 5 minutes, or until just tender. Remove with a slotted spoon and refresh the beans under cold running water. Drain and put into a large bowl.

Return the bean cooking water to a boil, add the pasta, and cook for 11 minutes, or until tender. Drain, return to the pan, and toss with the remaining oil.

Add the pasta to the beans with the onions, radicchio leaves, olives and hazelnuts. Transfer to a serving dish or salad bowl and arrange some thinly sliced beef on top.

Whisk the dressing ingredients together in a separate bowl, then pour over the salad and serve at once.

serves 2

3¹/2 oz/100 g small wholewheat pasta

2 tbsp olive oil

1 tbsp mayonnaise

1 tbsp plain yogurt

2 tbsp pesto

salt and pepper

7 oz/200 g canned tuna in spring water, drained and flaked

7 oz/200 g canned no-added-sugar corn kernels, drained

2 tomatoes, peeled, seeded, and chopped

¹/2 green bell pepper, seeded and chopped

¹/2 avocado, pitted, peeled, and chopped

pasta salad

Cook the pasta in a large pan of boiling water for 8–10 minutes until only just tender. Drain, return to the pan, and add half the oil. Toss well to coat, then cover and let cool.

Whisk the mayonnaise, yogurt, and pesto together in a pitcher, adding a little oil if needed to achieve the desired consistency. Add a pinch of salt and season to taste with pepper.

Mix the cooled pasta with the tuna, corn, tomatoes, green bell pepper, and avocado, add the dressing, and toss well to coat.

serves 4–6

2 tuna steaks, about
3/4 inch/2 cm thick

olive oil

salt and pepper

9 oz/250 g green beans,
trimmed

1 quantity garlic vinaigrette

2 hearts of lettuce,
leaves separated

3 large hard-cooked eggs,
cut into fourths

2 juicy vine-ripened
tomatoes, cut into wedges

1 3/4 oz/50 g anchovy fillets
in oil, drained

2 oz/55 g Niçoise olives

salad niçoise

Heat a ridged cast-iron grill pan over high heat until you can feel the heat rising from the surface. Brush the tuna steaks with oil, then place, oiled side down, on the hot pan and charbroil for 2 minutes.

Lightly brush the top side of the tuna steaks with a little more oil. Use a pair of tongs to turn the tuna steaks over, then season to taste with salt and pepper. Continue charbroiling for an additional 2 minutes for rare or up to 4 minutes for well done. Let cool.

Meanwhile, bring a pan of salted water to a boil. Add the beans to the pan and return to a boil, then boil for 3 minutes, or until tender-crisp. Drain the beans and immediately transfer them to a large bowl. Pour over the garlic vinaigrette and stir together, then let the beans cool in the dressing.

To serve, line a platter with lettuce leaves. Lift the beans out of the bowl, leaving the excess dressing behind, and pile them in the center of the platter. Break the tuna into large flakes and arrange it over the beans.

Arrange the hard-cooked eggs and tomatoes around the side. Place the anchovy fillets over the salad, then scatter with the olives. Drizzle the remaining dressing in the bowl over everything.

serves 4

2 ripe beefsteak tomatoes

5 1/2 oz/150 g fresh
mozzarella cheese

2 avocados

few fresh basil leaves,
torn into pieces

20 black olives

fresh crusty bread, to serve

for the dressing

4 tbsp olive oil

1 1/2 tbsp white wine vinegar

1 tsp coarse grain mustard

salt and pepper

tomato, mozzarella & avocado salad

Using a sharp knife, cut the tomatoes into thick wedges and place in a large serving dish. Drain the mozzarella cheese and coarsely tear into pieces. Cut the avocados in half, peel, and remove the pits. Cut the flesh into slices, then arrange the mozzarella cheese and avocado with the tomatoes.

Mix the oil, vinegar, and mustard together in a small bowl, add salt and pepper to taste, then drizzle over the salad.

Sprinkle the basil and olives over the top and serve at once with fresh crusty bread.

serves 4

4 tomatoes, cut into wedges

1 onion, sliced

1/2 cucumber, sliced

1 1/3 cups olives, pitted

8 oz/225 g feta cheese, cubed
(drained weight)

2 tbsp fresh cilantro leaves

fresh flat-leaf parsley,
to garnish

pita bread, to serve

for the dressing

5 tbsp extra virgin olive oil

2 tbsp white wine vinegar

1 tbsp lemon juice

1/2 tsp sugar

1 tbsp chopped fresh cilantro

salt and pepper

greek salad

To make the dressing, place the oil, vinegar, lemon juice, sugar, and cilantro in a large bowl. Season with salt and pepper and mix together well.

Add the tomatoes, onion, cucumber, olives, feta cheese, and cilantro. Toss all the ingredients together, then divide among individual serving bowls. Garnish with fresh parsley and serve with pita bread.

serves 4

1 large romaine lettuce or
2 Boston lettuces

4 canned anchovies in oil,
drained and halved
lengthwise

Parmesan shavings,
to garnish

for the dressing

2 garlic cloves, crushed

1½ tsp Dijon mustard

1 tsp Worcestershire sauce

4 canned anchovies in olive
oil, drained and chopped

1 egg yolk

1 tbsp lemon juice

salt and pepper

⅔ cup olive oil

4 tbsp Parmesan cheese
shavings

for the croutons

4 thick slices day-old bread

2 tbsp olive oil

1 garlic clove, crushed

caesar salad

Preheat the oven to 350°F/180°C. To make the dressing, place
the garlic, mustard, Worcestershire sauce, anchovies, egg yolk,
lemon juice, and salt and pepper to taste in a food processor
or blender and process for 30 seconds until foaming. With the
machine still running, add the olive oil, drop by drop, until the
mixture begins to thicken. Continue adding the oil in a steady
stream until all the oil has been incorporated. Transfer to a
bowl. Add a little hot water if the dressing is too thick. Stir in the
grated Parmesan cheese. Season to taste with salt and pepper
and let chill until required.

To make the croutons, cut the bread into 1/2-inch/1-cm cubes.
Toss with the oil and garlic in a bowl. Spread out on a baking
sheet in a single layer. Bake in the preheated oven for 15–20
minutes, stirring occasionally, until browned and crisp. Remove
from the oven and let cool.

Separate the lettuce into individual leaves and wash and spin
dry in a salad spinner or pat dry on paper towels. (Excess
moisture will dilute the dressing.) Transfer to a plastic bag and
place in the refrigerator.

To assemble the salad, tear the lettuce into pieces and place in
a large serving bowl. Add the dressing and toss well. Top with
the halved anchovies, croutons, and Parmesan cheese shavings.
Serve immediately.

serves 4

12 slices French bread

6 oz/175 g round goat cheese in a log, cut into 12 slices

4$\frac{1}{2}$ oz/125 g mixed salad greens, large ones torn into bite-sized pieces

2 tbsp snipped fresh chives

6 tbsp vinaigrette or garlic vinaigrette

pepper

broiled goat cheese salad

Preheat the broiler to high. Place the bread slices on a broiler rack and toast until crisp and golden but not dark brown. Immediately remove the broiler rack from under the broiler and turn the slices of toast over.

Place a slice of goat cheese on each bread slice, then return them to the broiler and broil for 2 minutes, or until the cheese is golden and bubbling.

Meanwhile, place the salad greens in a large bowl with the chives, then add the dressing of your choice and use your hands to toss until the leaves are coated.

Divide the salad among individual plates. Top each with 3 cheese-topped toasts and serve while still hot, seasoned with black pepper to taste.

serves 6

6 plum tomatoes, halved

1 red onion, cut into wedges

1 onion, cut into wedges

2 small zucchini, cut into chunks

1 eggplant, cut into chunks

1 red bell pepper, seeded and thickly sliced

5 tbsp olive oil

few fresh rosemary sprigs

few fresh thyme sprigs

1 tbsp rock salt

pepper

2 large tomatoes, coarsely chopped

roasted tomatoes with vegetables

Preheat the oven to 400°F/200°C. Place the plum tomatoes and vegetables on a large baking sheet and drizzle with oil.

Arrange the herbs on top, reserving one sprig of thyme for a garnish, and cook in the oven for 20–30 minutes. Toss the vegetables halfway through to coat with the oil. Season to taste with rock salt and pepper and cook for an additional 15–20 minutes, until the vegetables are tender and browned.

Remove the baking sheet from the oven, stir in the chopped tomatoes, garnish with the remaining thyme, and serve at once.

serves 4

3/4 cup long-grain white or brown rice

4 large red bell peppers

2 tbsp olive oil

1 garlic clove, chopped

4 shallots, chopped

1 celery stalk, chopped

3 tbsp chopped toasted walnuts

2 tomatoes, peeled and chopped

1 tbsp lemon juice

1/3 cup raisins

4 tbsp freshly grated Cheddar cheese

2 tbsp chopped fresh basil

salt and pepper

fresh basil sprigs, to garnish

lemon wedges, to serve

stuffed red bell peppers with basil

Preheat the oven to 350°F/180°C. Cook the rice in a pan of lightly salted boiling water for 20 minutes if using white rice, or 35 minutes if using brown. Drain, rinse under cold running water, then drain again.

Using a sharp knife, cut the tops off the bell peppers and set aside. Remove the seeds and white cores, then blanch the bell peppers and reserved tops in boiling water for 2 minutes. Remove from the heat and drain well. Heat half the oil in a large skillet. Add the garlic and shallots and cook, stirring, for 3 minutes. Add the celery, walnuts, tomatoes, lemon juice, and raisins and cook for an additional 5 minutes. Remove from the heat and stir in the cheese, chopped basil, rice, and seasoning.

Stuff the bell peppers with the rice mixture and arrange them in a baking dish. Place the tops on the bell peppers, drizzle over the remaining oil, loosely cover with foil, and bake in the preheated oven for 45 minutes. Remove from the oven. Garnish with basil sprigs and serve with lemon wedges.

Ladies who Lunch

serves 4

4 boneless chicken breasts,
about 6 oz/175 g each

salt and pepper

1/4 stick unsalted butter

1 tbsp sunflower-seed oil

for the tarragon sauce

2 tbsp tarragon-flavored
vinegar

6 tbsp dry white wine, such
as Muscadet

1 cup chicken stock

4 sprigs fresh tarragon, plus
2 tbsp chopped fresh tarragon

1 1/4 cups sour cream or
heavy cream

new potatoes, to serve

chicken in tarragon sauce

Preheat the oven to 375°F/190°C. Season the chicken breasts on both sides with salt and pepper.

Melt the butter with the oil in a sauté pan or skillet large enough to hold the chicken pieces in a single layer, over medium-high heat. Add the chicken breasts, skin-side down, and sauté for 3–5 minutes, or until golden brown.

Transfer the chicken breasts to a roasting pan and roast for 15–20 minutes, or until they are tender and the juices run clear when a skewer is inserted into the thickest part of the meat. Transfer the chicken to a serving platter and cover with foil, shiny-side down, then set aside.

To make the tarragon sauce, tilt the roasting pan and use a large metal spoon to remove the excess fat from the surface of the cooking juices. Place the roasting pan over medium-high heat and add the vinegar, scraping any sediment from the bottom of the tin. Pour in the wine and bring to a boil, still stirring and scraping, and boil until the liquid is reduced by half.

Stir in the stock and whole tarragon sprigs and continue boiling until the liquid reduces to about 1/2 cup.

Stir in the sour cream and continue boiling to reduce the sauce by half. Discard the tarragon sprigs, and adjust the seasoning if necessary. Stir the chopped tarragon into the sauce.

To serve, slice the chicken breasts on individual plates and spoon a quarter of the sauce over each. Serve with freshly cooked new potatoes.

serves 4

4 rump, sirloin, or tenderloin steaks, about 6–8 oz/ 175–225 g each and 1 inch/ 2.5 cm thick

pepper

olive or sunflower-seed oil, for pan-frying

1 tbsp butter, for pan-frying

fresh watercress sprigs, to garnish

French fries (see page 51) and crispy onion rings, to serve

for the béarnaise sauce

4 tbsp white wine or tarragon vinegar

1 shallot, finely chopped

2 fresh tarragon sprigs plus 1 tbsp finely chopped fresh tarragon

2 egg yolks

6 tbsp butter, softened

salt and pepper

pan-fried steaks with béarnaise sauce

First make the sauce. Put the vinegar, shallot, and tarragon sprigs into a small, heavy-bottom pan over medium-low heat and let simmer until reduced to 1 tablespoon. Let cool.

Strain the vinegar mixture into a heatproof bowl set over a pan of simmering water. Add the egg yolks and whisk together until thick.

Gradually add the butter in small pieces, whisking after each addition, until combined and the sauce has thickened. Add the chopped tarragon and season to taste with salt and pepper.

Cover the surface of the sauce with a piece of dampened wax paper to prevent a skin from forming. Remove from the heat, but leave over the pan of hot water to keep hot while you cook the steaks.

Season the steaks to taste with pepper. Heat a film of oil in a large, heavy-bottom skillet over high heat. When hot, add the butter, and as soon as it has melted, add the steaks. Cook quickly on both sides to seal, then reduce the heat to medium and cook, turning once, for 2½–3 minutes each side for rare, 3½–5 minutes each side for medium, and 5–7 minutes each side for well done.

Serve the steaks at once, with the Béarnaise sauce, French fries and crispy onion rings.

serves 4

6 cups fresh baby spinach leaves

2 tbsp olive oil

5$^1/_2$ oz/150 g pancetta cubetti

10 oz/280 g mixed wild mushrooms, sliced

for the dressing

5 tbsp olive oil

1 tbsp balsamic vinegar

1 tsp Dijon mustard

pinch of sugar

salt and pepper

warm mushroom, spinach & pancetta salad

To make the dressing, place the olive oil, vinegar, mustard, sugar, salt, and pepper in a small bowl and whisk together.

Rinse the baby spinach under cold running water, then drain and place in a large salad bowl.

Heat the oil in a large skillet. Add the pancetta and cook for 3 minutes. Add the mushrooms and cook for 3–4 minutes, or until tender.

Pour the dressing into the skillet and immediately turn the cooked mixture and dressing into the bowl with the spinach. Toss until coated with the dressing and serve at once.

serves 4

1 eggplant

salt and pepper

4–8 lamb chops

3 tbsp olive oil

1 onion, chopped coarsely

1 garlic clove, chopped finely

14 oz canned chopped tomatoes in juice

pinch of sugar

16 black olives, pitted and chopped coarsely

1 tsp chopped fresh herbs such as basil, flat-leaf parsley, or oregano

lamb with eggplant

Cut the eggplant into ¾-inch cubes, put in a colander standing over a large plate, and sprinkle each layer with salt. Cover with another plate and place a heavy weight on top. Leave for 30 minutes.

Preheat the broiler. Rinse the eggplant slices under cold running water, then pat dry with paper towels. Season the lamb chops with pepper.

Place the lamb chops on the broiler pan and cook under medium heat for 10–15 minutes until tender, turning once during the cooking time.

Meanwhile, heat the olive oil in a saucepan, add the eggplant, onion, and garlic, and fry for 10 minutes, until softened and starting to brown. Add the tomatoes and their juice, the sugar, olives, chopped herbs, salt, and pepper and simmer for 5–10 minutes.

To serve, spoon the sauce onto four warmed serving plates and top with the lamb chops.

serves 4

4 salmon fillets, about 7 oz/200 g each

1/2 cup teriyaki marinade

1 shallot, sliced

3/4-inch/2-cm piece fresh gingerroot, finely chopped

2 carrots, sliced

4 oz/115 g closed-cup mushrooms, sliced

5 cups vegetable stock

9 oz/250 g dried medium egg noodles

1 cup frozen peas

6 oz/175 g Napa cabbage, shredded

4 scallions, sliced

teriyaki salmon fillets with chinese noodles

Wipe off any scales from the salmon skin. Arrange the salmon fillets, skin-side up, in a dish just large enough to fit them in a single layer. Mix the teriyaki marinade with the shallot and ginger in a small bowl and pour over the salmon. Cover and let marinate in the refrigerator for at least 1 hour, turning the salmon over halfway through the marinating time.

Put the carrots, mushrooms, and stock into a large pan. Arrange the salmon, skin-side down, on a shallow baking sheet. Pour the fish marinade into the pan of vegetables and stock and bring to a boil. Reduce the heat, cover, and let simmer for 10 minutes.

Meanwhile, preheat the broiler to medium. Cook the salmon under the preheated broiler for 10–15 minutes, depending on the thickness of the fillets, until the flesh turns pink and flakes easily. Remove from the broiler and keep warm.

Add the noodles and peas to the stock and return to a boil. Reduce the heat, cover, and let simmer for 5 minutes, or until the noodles are tender. Stir in the Napa cabbage and scallions and heat through for 1 minute.

Carefully drain off 1¼ cups of the stock into a small heatproof pitcher and set aside. Drain and discard the remaining stock. Divide the noodles and vegetables among 4 warmed serving bowls and top each with a salmon fillet. Pour the reserved stock over each meal and serve at once.

serves 4

1 tbsp each dried thyme,
dried rosemary, dried
oregano, and mild paprika

1 tsp garlic powder

2 tsp cumin seeds

1 tbsp sea salt

4 salmon fillets,
skin removed

1 tbsp vegetable oil

scant 3 1/2 cups baby spinach

for the hollandaise sauce

3 egg yolks

7 oz/200 g butter

1 tbsp lemon juice

pepper

seared salmon with quick hollandaise sauce & baby spinach

Combine the dried herbs, paprika, garlic powder, cumin seeds, and sea salt in a small grinder and process until smooth. Alternatively, grind by hand using a pestle in a mortar. Rub 1 tablespoon of the mixture into the top of each of the salmon fillets.

Heat the oil in a large skillet and cook the salmon, spice-side down, for 2–3 minutes, or until golden brown. Turn over and continue cooking until the salmon is cooked to your liking. Do not overcook or the salmon will be dry.

To make the hollandaise sauce, place the egg yolks in a food processor. Melt the butter in a small pan until bubbling. With the motor running, gradually add the hot butter in a steady stream until the sauce is thick and creamy. Add the lemon juice, and a little warm water if the sauce is too thick, then season to taste with pepper. Remove from the food processor and keep warm.

Divide the baby spinach equally among 4 plates, place the cooked salmon on top, and spoon over the sauce. Serve at once.

serves 4

4 fresh tuna steaks, about
3/4-inch/2-cm thick

olive oil

salt and pepper

lemon wedges, to serve

for the green sauce

2 oz/55 g fresh flat-leaf
parsley, leaves and stems

4 scallions, chopped

2 garlic cloves, chopped

3 anchovy fillets in oil,
drained

1 oz/30 g fresh basil leaves

1/2 tbsp capers in brine,
rinsed and dried

2 sprigs of fresh oregano or
1/2 tsp dried oregano

1/2 cup extra-virgin olive oil,
plus extra for brushing the
tuna

1–2 tbsp lemon juice, to taste

tuna with green sauce

To make the green sauce, put the parsley, scallions, garlic, anchovy fillets, basil, capers, and oregano in a food processor. Pulse to chop and blend together. With the motor still running, pour in the oil through the feed tube. Add lemon juice to taste, then whizz again. If the sauce is too thick, add a little extra oil. Cover and chill until required.

Place a ridged cast-iron skillet over high heat until you can feel the heat rising from the surface. Brush the tuna steaks with oil and place, oiled-side down, on the hot pan and charbroil for 2 minutes.

Lightly brush the top side of the tuna steaks with a little more oil. Use a pair of tongs to turn the tuna steaks over, then season to taste with salt and pepper. Continue charbroiling for an additional 2 minutes for rare or up to 4 minutes for well done.

Transfer the tuna steaks to serving plates and serve with lemon wedges and the green sauce spooned over.

serves 4

3 tbsp olive oil

2 garlic cloves, chopped finely

10 anchovy fillets, drained and chopped

scant 1 cup black olives, pitted and chopped

1 tbsp capers, rinsed

1 lb plum tomatoes, peeled, seeded, and chopped

pinch of cayenne pepper

salt

14 oz dried linguine

2 tbsp chopped fresh flat-leaf parsley, to garnish

linguine with anchovies, olives & capers

Heat the olive oil in a heavy-bottom pan. Add the garlic and cook over low heat, stirring frequently, for 2 minutes. Add the anchovies and mash them to a pulp with a fork. Add the olives, capers, and tomatoes and season to taste with cayenne pepper. Cover and let simmer for 25 minutes.

Meanwhile, bring a pan of lightly salted water to a boil. Add the pasta, bring back to a boil, and cook for 8–10 minutes, until tender but still firm to the bite. Drain and transfer to a warmed serving dish.

Spoon the anchovy sauce into the dish and toss the pasta, using 2 large forks. Garnish with the parsley and serve immediately.

makes 12

3/4 cup buckwheat flour

3/4 cup white bread flour

1/4 oz/7 g sachet active
dry yeast

1 tsp salt

scant 1 3/4 cups tepid milk

2 eggs, 1 whole and
1 separated

vegetable oil, for brushing

sour cream, smoked salmon
and lemon wedges, to serve

pepper

blinis with smoked salmon

Sift both flours into a large, warmed bowl. Stir in the yeast and salt. Beat in the milk, whole egg, and egg yolk until smooth. Cover the bowl and let stand in a warm place for 1 hour.

Place the egg white in a spotlessly clean bowl and whisk until soft peaks form. Fold into the batter. Brush a heavy-bottom skillet with oil and set over medium-high heat. When the skillet is hot, pour enough of the batter onto the surface to make a blini about the size of a saucer.

When bubbles rise, turn the blini over with a spatula and cook the other side until light brown. Wrap in a clean dish towel to keep warm while cooking the remainder. Serve the warm blinis with sour cream, smoked salmon, and lemon wedges and season with pepper.

serves 4

1 lb 5 oz/600 g butternut squash or pumpkin, peeled and cut into bite-size pieces

4 tbsp olive oil

1 tsp honey

2 tbsp fresh basil

2 tbsp fresh oregano

1 tbsp margarine

2 onions, finely chopped

1 lb/450 g risotto rice

3/4 cup dry white wine

5 cups hot vegetable stock

salt and pepper

roasted butternut squash risotto

Preheat the oven to 400°F/200°C. Put the squash into a roasting pan. Mix 1 tablespoon of the oil with the honey and spoon over the squash. Turn the squash to coat it in the mixture. Roast in the preheated oven for 30–35 minutes, or until tender.

Meanwhile, put the basil and oregano into a food processor with 2 tablespoons of the remaining oil and process until finely chopped and blended. Set aside.

Heat the margarine and remaining oil in a large, heavy-bottom pan over medium heat. Add the onions and cook, stirring occasionally, for 8 minutes, or until soft and golden. Add the rice and cook for 2 minutes, stirring to coat the grains in the oil mixture.

Pour in the wine and bring to a boil. Reduce the heat slightly and cook until the wine is almost absorbed. Add the stock, a little at a time, and cook over medium-low heat, stirring constantly, for 20 minutes.

Gently stir in the herb oil and squash until thoroughly mixed into the rice and cook for an additional 5 minutes, or until the rice is creamy and cooked but retaining a little bite in the center of the grain. Season well with salt and pepper before serving.